www.ingramcontent.com/pod-product-compliance
Lightning Source LLC
Chambersburg PA
CBHW031138090426
42738CB00008B/1137

Finding
My Own Truth

ELIZABETH RICHARDS ADAMS

ASA PUBLISHING CORPORATION
AN INNOVATIVE OUTSOURCE BOOK PUBLISHING HYBRID

ASA Publishing Corporation
1285 N. Telegraph Rd., #351, Monroe, Michigan 48162
An Accredited Publishing House with the BBB
www.asapublishingcorporation.com

All Rights Reserved. No part of this publication may be reproduced, stored in a retrieval system or transmitted in any form or by any means electronic, mechanical, photocopying, recording or otherwise, without the prior written permission of the publisher. Author/writer rights to "Freedom of Speech" protected by and with the "1st Amendment" of the Constitution of the United States of America. This is a work of non-fiction; an autobiographical encouragement novel. Any resemblance to actual events, locales, person living or deceased that is not related to the author's literacy is entirely coincidental.

With this title/copyrights page, the reader is notified that the publisher does not assume, and expressly disclaims any obligation to obtain and/or include any other information other than that provided by the author, except with permission. Any belief system, or promotional motivations, including but not limited to the use of non-fictional/fictional characters and/or characteristics of this book, are within the boundaries of the author's own creativity in order to reflect the nature and concept of the book. Unauthorized printing is prohibited to avoid counterfeit books and plagiarism.

Any and all vending sales and distribution are not permitted without full book cover and this title page.
Copyrights©2025, Elizabeth Richards Adams, All Rights Reserved.
Book Title: Finding My Own Truth
Date Published: 12.23.2025
Book ID: ASAPCID2380974
Edition: 1 *Trade Paperback*
ISBN: 978-1-960104-97-7
Library of Congress Cataloging-in-Publication Data

This book was published in the United States of America.
Great State of Michigan

Dedication

To my inner little girl. The little girl that felt invisible. You did it Liz!

"No regrets live here!"

I also dedicate this book to my children, my jewels. Sabrina (an authentic walking universe), Zolo (Creator self made), and Lateef (Legend). I love you all the same and I will create an example of going after your dreams and making them a reality.

To my husband, who is my loving and supportive partner.

"I Love Your Heart"

Table of Contents

Introduction .... (A)
About the Author .... (C)

Chapter 1
   The Beginning of My Truth 3

Chapter 2
   The Little Girl, the Woman, and Family 13

Chapter 3
   Finding My Own Truth 25

Chapter 4
   Mind, Trauma, and Self-Sabotage 39

Chapter 5
   Body, Identity, and Killing the Old Self 53

Chapter 6
   Love, Kingship, and Partnership 63

Chapter 7
   Decompression, Awakening, and Epiphanies 73

Chapter 8
   Channeling My Own Frequency 89

Paintings by Elizabeth
   These Paintings 99

Introduction

Finding My Own Truth by Elizabeth Richards Adams is a deeply personal and transformative memoir that explores the journey of self-discovery, healing, and spiritual awakening. Through raw honesty and introspection, Elizabeth shares her experiences of overcoming trauma, breaking generational cycles, and reclaiming her voice.

The chapters in this book reflect pivotal moments in her life, from confronting childhood wounds to embracing her identity as a woman shaped by resilience and growth. Elizabeth delves into themes of self-sabotage, spiritual deconstruction, emotional healing, and the power of choosing authenticity over societal expectations.

With heartfelt letters to her younger self, reflections on love and partnership, and insights into spiritual alignment, Elizabeth invites readers to embark on their own journey of transformation. Her story is a testament to the power of vulnerability, self-awareness, and the courage to embrace change.

Accompanied by her evocative paintings, *Finding My*

Own Truth is not just a memoir but a guide for anyone seeking to rise above pain, rediscover their inner strength, and live in alignment with their true frequency. It is a celebration of growth, freedom, and the beauty of becoming.

So, let's dive into *Finding My Own Truth* . . .

About the Author

Elizabeth Richards Adams

Born in Gary Indiana and had lived a very struggled life without siblings because they all grew up and left the nest. The author also grew up in a single mother home being the last child of ten children – she felt like her existence was like a ghost. Being that she was never heard, Elizabeth always felt that she was never enough.

The author became a young wife and mother to a pastor, and that's when she found herself asking questions. Questions that took her beyond her own teachings from her environment into an understanding of who she is, and the woman she began to fall in love with.

Enjoy this memoir of Elizabeth Richards Adams, *Finding My Own Truth*.

Finding
My Own Truth

ELIZABETH RICHARDS ADAMS

CHAPTER 1

The Beginning of My Truth

"When a woman begins to hear her own inner voice, the world has no choice but to shift around her." — Unknown

Every story begins with a moment when truth becomes louder than fear. For Elizabeth, this chapter marks the awakening of a woman who had spent years carrying responsibilities, expectations, and silent wounds. Before the transformation came the stirring. The quiet recognition that life as she knew it no longer fit the woman she was becoming. This section opens the door to the earliest whispers of her evolution: the first steps toward reclaiming her voice.

The Beginning

I started writing at a time when I felt full but directionless, carrying stories, memories, and emotions that had nowhere to go. In my self-reflection, I began to notice how many opportunities I'd turned away from because of fear. Fear can hold you hostage in your own life. It convinces you that playing small is safer, even when you know you're meant for more. I always knew I was supposed to impact the world, yet I kept wrestling with procrastination like it was stitched into my spirit.

For years, I poured everything into my children and the men I loved, but I rarely poured into myself. Spiritually, I felt connected to God, as if He and I were finally understanding one another. Still, a part of me felt out of alignment, especially after years of being a First Lady. Something inside me resisted the teachings I was expected to accept. I often woke up from dreams that felt like divine messages, but I twisted them through the lens of Christianity and missed what my spirit was trying to say.

I still read the Bible, but I don't practice everything within it, and that honesty will unfold throughout this book. Transformation is uncomfortable for many of us, especially when the old version of ourselves begins to disagree with the new one trying to evolve. One morning, I woke up and noticed my patterns, habits I repeated out of survival rather than purpose. Life teaches us patterns, but some of them become cages.

Bondage feels like a hopelessness you can't name. It's a heaviness that presses into your chest, making you question your worth. Yet that same morning, I felt something different. My vibration rose, and a creative energy sat on me gently, like a dove settling onto a branch. Painting became an outlet, but I was terrified to show my work. My art was me, and if someone rejected it, it felt like they were rejecting the deepest part of who I was.

I used to sit in silence, staring at my paintings as if they were mirrors asking me to see myself fully. The truth was simple but hard: I needed to become my own validation. I had to stop depending on others to tell me I mattered. I remember sitting in my car listening to Cleo Sol's "Know That You Are Loved," realizing how often I had settled in relationships. I accepted things that made me uncomfortable just to avoid rocking the boat.

That frustration grew into a truth I could no longer ignore: I wasn't living the life I felt I deserved. I was living the life I thought I was stuck with.

Healing became necessary. Survival no longer felt enough. Everything I had been holding back began to transform into a calling. A higher version of myself asking to be born.

A Shift Within

As that new awareness grew, I began noticing how often I abandoned myself. I had been living in fragments, showing pieces of who I was while hiding the parts that needed nurturing. Transformation is not a single moment; it's a shift that starts quietly, almost unnoticeably. It asks you to tell the truth about who you are and who you are becoming.

Sometimes that truth is beautiful, and sometimes it stings.

I realized that healing doesn't happen in perfect order. It happens in waves. Some soft, some crashing, some flooding everything you thought you knew. And when the wave hits, you don't get to run. You have to let it wash over you so it can reveal what needs to be rebuilt.

This was my rebuilding.

My Truth

I have always been someone who starts things but struggles to finish them. My mind moves fast, jumping from thought to thought as if inspiration has a short attention span. I used to wonder why I was wired this way, why the overthinking felt louder than my own voice. I would start a task with excitement, then shift into another idea before I could finish the first. I'm an innovative woman, full of creativity, but expressing all of it at once became overwhelming.

When I finally gained a clearer understanding of the woman I was becoming, I grew afraid of my own potential. Seeing my value scared me because I had never been taught how to embrace it. Success comes with responsibility, and responsibility comes with pressure. I danced in my fear until reality checked me, forcing me to confront the child inside me who still needed healing.

Boundaries became necessary. I had to learn them unapologetically. So many of us punish ourselves more than life ever could. We sentence ourselves to small thinking, small relationships, and small dreams. But I want to speak to the King and Queen in whoever reads this:

You are enough. Your obstacles were not designed to break you; they were meant to build your worth.

When I looked up the definition of worth:

"the level at which someone or something deserves to be valued"

I realized that the word *deserves* was the one holding me hostage. I didn't feel deserving. I chose friendships, relationships, and environments that matched the low value I'd assigned to myself.

My ancestors, my parents, tried to redirect me, but I didn't listen. Instead, I punished myself through the choices I made. I couldn't see my greatness because I used my story as an excuse, clinging to the narrative that pain was all I deserved.

Society tells us that being "awoke" is trendy, yet many who preach self-love seek validation online. In my generation, being "awoke" was seen as witchcraft; meditation, yoga, and silence were labeled "demonic." But I had to question: *Who made those rules? Who benefits from keeping people disconnected from themselves?*

So I looked up the word perception: "The ability to see, hear, or become aware of something through the senses."

And the truth hit me. If you've never seen a healthy marriage, how can you know how to be a spouse?

If you've never seen healthy parenting, how can you model it?

Transformation begins when you divorce the beliefs that never belonged to you. It's messy, uncomfortable, and necessary.

When we are born, we know nothing. We come into the world pure. Life layers us with experiences, traumas, expectations, and mistakes. Eventually, we must return to a rebirthing stage. A stage where we choose who we are outside of the noise.

You are loved. You have the ability to be free within yourself.

Freedom is sacred. You know you've reached it when no one can disturb your peace. You don't have to overexplain yourself to be understood. You don't have to shrink yourself to be accepted.

Returning to the Beginning

Healing forced me to return to the beginning of my story. It felt like a referee throwing a flag in a football game, saying, "Start over. Go back to where it began." I had been running through life thinking I was winning, only to realize parts of me were still wounded and unheard.

I am not a product of my environment. My environment was an assignment. a place designed to prepare me for where I am destined to be.

It was the Universe shaping me for what was coming.

Healing doesn't happen all at once; it unfolds in layers. As Elizabeth began to understand herself as a woman, she realized she also needed to reach back to the girl who never had the chance to be seen. That next chapter of her journey required revisiting the beginning. Not to relive the pain, but to finally embrace the child who needed her.

CHAPTER 2

The Little Girl, the Woman, and Family

"Childhood isn't where we stay—it's where we start." — Cleo Sol

Who we become as adults is deeply entangled with who we were as children. This chapter reflects Elizabeth's return to the tender, wounded parts of herself. The little girl who carried silence, shame, gifts, and grief long before she understood their weight. Here, she reconnects with that younger version of herself to give her the voice, validation, and compassion she never received.

The Letter to My Little Girl

Dear little girl. The skinny one who later became chubby and learned to hide her own body in shame. I never gave you the chance you truly deserved. I let my own low self-esteem spill into your childhood, shaping how you saw yourself long before you understood what self-worth even was. I wished so deeply for a different family, a different beginning, that I didn't notice I was abandoning you in the process. I apologize for every moment I didn't allow you to believe in yourself. I'm sorry for letting our parents' words make you feel insufficient, like you were never enough no matter how hard you tried.

I'm sorry for the times Daddy made you feel bothersome, as if your voice was something he tolerated rather than cherished. You were the baby of the family, but no one ever truly heard you. You screamed silently, hoping someone would care enough to understand the words you couldn't speak out loud. I apologize for every talent I did not nurture; your voice, your creativity, your imagination. All of those gifts were real and powerful, and they deserved to be seen and protected.

There were so many moments when you didn't feel accepted, when not fitting in made you think something was wrong with you. You didn't know then that being different was a blessing. I am crying for you even now as I remember the day you held Mom in your arms at sixteen and watched her take her last breath. You got stuck there, frozen in grief, suspended between childhood and adulthood. You were angry with God, confused, heartbroken, and trying to carry a loss that no sixteen-year-old should ever have to endure.

But hear me clearly: you were never alone. Even when Mom didn't understand every part of you, she believed in your gifts. I need you to wipe the tears of disappointment that others caused you. Their inability to see your beauty, worth, and light was never a reflection of you.

>Little girl, listen closely:
>You are beautiful.
>You are enough.
>You are gifted.

You are not a burden.
You are loved.

Growing Up in the Middle of Dysfunction

Growing up, I didn't have the emotional tools to protect the little girl inside me. Instead, I carried her wounds like invisible weight, dragging them into every room I entered as a woman. My environment wasn't nurturing, it was survival-based. I learned early that love could be inconsistent, emotions could be unpredictable, and the people who were supposed to teach me security were battling their own storms.

My mother was a complicated woman, soft in some moments and hurting in others. She carried sadness the way some people carry perfume: Constantly present, even when she smiled. My father loved us the best way he knew how, but emotional connection wasn't one of his strengths. He wasn't unkind; he was unavailable. That silence shaped me more than his words ever could. It taught me to read rooms, overanalyze reactions, and anticipate disappointment before it arrived.

Dysfunction became my normal. I didn't know what healthy communication looked like because I never saw it. Tenderness felt foreign. Safety felt temporary. And because I grew up with emotional gaps, I learned to fill them with perfectionism, people-pleasing, and silence. These were survival mechanisms, but I carried them long after I stopped needing them. They followed me into friendships, relationships, motherhood, and even the way I loved myself.

I became a woman built from broken pieces, trying to create a life that made sense while healing wounds I didn't fully understand. It took years to realize that dysfunction wasn't my foundation, it was simply my starting point. The woman I became had to learn love differently. She had to rewrite what connection looked like, relearn what boundaries meant, and reshape what she believed she deserved.

My Narrative (Wanna Be Loved)

My narrative was never the fairytale people imagine. Girl meets boy, they fall in love, get married, have three kids, and live happily ever after. That's the story many young women are conditioned to expect, but it was never mine. Growing up, I wanted luxury, travel, and even fame. Building a family wasn't part of my early dreams because I had no example of a healthy family structure. By the time I was ten, my siblings were gone, and it was just me and my sister in the house.

I watched struggle so closely that it became something I feared repeating. Watching my mother raise us alone while carrying so much sadness made me terrified of becoming a single mother. Yet the very thing I feared became my reality. Life has a way of handing you the lessons you try to avoid. I became a single mother and had to play both roles. Provider and nurturer, disciplinarian and comforter. That duality hardened me. I developed a tough exterior when all I truly wanted was softness.

My family was dysfunctional, not because they were bad people, but because they were broken people. My father didn't know how to express emotions, especially toward his daughters. My mother loved deeply but carried wounds that were never healed. So how was I supposed to build healthy relationships when love, communication, and softness were foreign languages to me? Naturally, I gravitated toward individuals, mostly men and friends, who had a hard time expressing themselves. Their emotional unavailability felt familiar, almost comfortable.

But when I took a real self-check, I realized something powerful: My life wasn't a nightmare. It was a narrative filled with battles meant to shape me, not destroy me.

Every struggle was preparing me for the woman I was becoming. It was all about perception, or how you see the world, and how you allow the world to shape how you see yourself.

The Woman I Became

As I grew, I became a woman stitched together by experiences that forced me to mature before I was ready. I learned how to survive heartbreak, loss, disappointment, and loneliness. I learned to navigate life without a blueprint, building myself while raising children at the same time. Survival became my specialty, even when I desperately wanted to experience life beyond survival mode.

The woman I became was strong, but also tired. She was resilient, but also burdened by expectations she never asked for. She knew how to fight, but didn't always know how to rest. She carried the weight of her past like a backpack filled with stones. Guilt, shame, responsibility, fear, and the haunting feeling of never being enough.

And yet, she grew.
She evolved.
She kept going.

Part of becoming this woman meant confronting the internalized beliefs I carried since childhood. I had to accept that my parents gave what they could, but they were limited by their own pain. I had to understand that their shortcomings did not define my worth. I had to separate inherited trauma from personal truth.

I began learning love differently, from

my mistakes, my reflections, and my healing. I learned that vulnerability wasn't weakness, but courage. I learned that receiving love required the same strength as giving it. I learned that family doesn't always mean closeness; sometimes it means understanding people from a distance while protecting your peace.

The woman I became had to decide whether she would keep repeating generational patterns or break them. And breaking them meant choosing healing even when it hurt.

My Children Were Never My Way Out

My children were never my escape from my past. They were the reason I had to confront it. They were my motivation to heal, to grow, and to become the mother they deserved. For years, I carried guilt like a second skin. Even after my children grew up, the guilt lingered. One day, one of them looked at me and said, "Mom, you always try to over-explain yourself when we've already forgiven you."

That moment stopped me. It taught me that forgiving myself was the hardest part of motherhood. We make mistakes as parents. Things we regret, moments we replay, decisions we wish we had done differently. But mistakes don't define us unless we refuse to grow from them.

My children watched me break down, rebuild myself, fall in love, lose myself, and rise again. They watched me struggle in relationships, lose my footing, and try to navigate pain while still trying to be their mother. They saw my strength, but they also saw my vulnerability. And even when I thought I was failing, they saw me trying.

My children were my why. They became my reason for breaking the generational curses that kept our family in cycles of religion without relationship, love without boundaries, survival without nourishment, and self-hate disguised as humility. As a mother, I carried guilt like a backpack, heavy and unnecessary. Over time, I realized I didn't have to carry it anymore. I can't change what happened, but I can control how I move now. I can choose healing. I can choose softness. I can choose growth.

And choosing those things for myself has allowed me to give them to my children, too.

Understanding her childhood brought clarity, but clarity often reveals deeper questions. As Elizabeth stepped into womanhood, she began to examine the systems, beliefs, and societal programming that shaped her thinking. Her journey was no longer just personal. It became spiritual.

CHAPTER 3

Noise, Programming, and Spiritual Deconstruction

"The quieter you become, the more you can hear." — Ram Dass

There comes a moment when the external world becomes too loud to ignore. The voices, expectations, traditions, and inherited beliefs that bury our intuition. Elizabeth's spiritual deconstruction began not with rebellion, but with honesty. This chapter explores the noise that shaped her and the awakening that freed her.

The Noise

The mornings have always been sacred for me. There is a harmony between my mind, my heart, and my spirit that only appears when things are still. When the world is sleeping and my thoughts have space to breathe, I can hear myself clearly. My prayers in those moments are quiet, not spoken out loud but whispered through my spirit. It is the kneeling of my inner self that brings me closer to truth. That is why I call this section "the noise". Because to understand peace, you must first understand what disrupts it.

In life, there is a part of us that constantly feels the need to explain ourselves or be understood. Everybody wants to be understood in some way. But striving to be understood can become draining when the wrong people are listening. The quiet becomes sacred because it creates space for focus, reflection, and grounding. In silence, there is room to hear yourself without the world trying to speak over you. Silence is where transformation begins.

I've never been a fan of people who need

noise around them constantly. It feels like they're trying to silence their own thoughts. When you fear your own mind, you distract yourself with sound, entertainment, or chaos. Noise becomes a coping mechanism. But the truth is, we have three forms of noise: the noise in our thoughts, the noise from the people we surround ourselves with, and the noise of society. All three can shape us, and all three can destroy us if we aren't careful.

We operate in an energy of self, and that energy can be fragile during transformation. When any of these forms of noise intrude during your healing, they can disrupt what the Universe is trying to help you rebuild. Becoming an enemy of your own thoughts is the first step toward becoming an enemy of yourself. That is why it's important to be mindful of not just what we hear, but who we hear it from. Some voices were never meant to guide us.

The Cost of Being Awake

Waking up spiritually, emotionally, or mentally is not as glamorous as people make it sound. There is a cost to awareness. When you begin hearing your own thoughts clearly, you also begin hearing the lies you once believed. When you start to see the world for what it truly is, you must also see yourself, your patterns, your wounds, your illusions. Awakening is not just light; it is confrontation.

Most people are not afraid of the truth itself; they are afraid of what the truth demands. If you know better, you must do better. If you see differently, you must live differently. And if you awaken, you can never again hide behind ignorance. Being awake means being intentional about every thought, every relationship, and every space you allow yourself to occupy. The cost is responsibility, and not everyone is ready for that.

When I began waking up, I felt separated from people I once felt close to. Their conversations felt shallow. Their interests felt different. Their values no longer aligned with my spirit. Some people stay asleep because sleep keeps them comfortable. But for me, discomfort became my teacher. Awakening forced me to walk away from noise, distractions, and programming that no longer served me. And in that separation, I found something priceless. Clarity.

The world doesn't reward awakening. It punishes it. People will call you crazy, rebellious, or "too deep" simply because you are no longer willing to be programmed. But that is the cost of choosing yourself. That is the cost of freedom.

Brainwashed Cult-Like Thinking

I've always had questions sitting in the back of my mind, even as a child. But in my generation, asking questions was seen as disrespectful. We were taught to follow, not think. We were told to believe without understanding and obey without clarity. That mentality became a kind of cult-like thinking. Tradition over truth, silence over curiosity. When I became a mother, I refused to pass that mindset on to my children. I taught them that questioning is healthy, and researching is necessary. Blind obedience breeds confusion.

Many people are comfortable being

controlled because belonging feels safer than independence. When you've never truly belonged anywhere, you might think I would have clung to any group that offered acceptance. But intuition kept me from following crowds just for comfort. Something deep inside me always whispered, *"Everything you see is not what it seems."* And I learned to trust that voice.

Now society has become hypnotized by technology. Social media, reels, trends. They've turned into tools of distraction and manipulation. People are no longer seeing truth; they are seeing what they are shown. We are fed narratives, aesthetics, opinions, and illusions that are designed to program how we think. The scariest part is that most people don't even realize they're under a spell. They defend the very systems that keep them limited.

You cannot know what is real unless you've awakened to your own spiritual frequency. There is a realm of truth hidden from the physical world. A spiritual realm where awareness is not optional, it's required.

Only those who tap into that spiritual side can feel the difference between what's real and what's manufactured. That realm is where God, angels, and spiritual entities operate. It's where intuition is born.

My spiritual deconstruction came from asking questions Christians could never answer. Any time I asked for clarity, someone became defensive. How could a God of love preach that love has no record of wrongs, yet still send people to burn for eternity? How could a Bible that claims God frees His people also degrade women as less valuable than men? Why did freedom come with so many conditions? As a parent, I would never let one of my own children suffer eternal punishment for disobedience. So why would a loving God do that?

The contradictions became too loud to ignore. So I stepped away from religion. Not from God, but from the structures created around Him. Religion taught fear. Spirit taught truth. And truth, for me, was freeing.

The Spiritual Unlearning

Unlearning is one of the hardest spiritual tasks. When you've been conditioned your entire life to see the world through a specific lens, letting go of that perspective feels like betrayal. But unlearning is not betrayal. It is liberation. It is peeling away beliefs that never belonged to you. It is dismantling the voice in your head that repeats generational patterns. It is clearing space for a new foundation.

Unlearning requires courage. It asks you to confront the illusion of certainty and step into the unknown. It forces you to examine what was taught, who taught it, and whether it aligns with your spirit. Most people fear this because unlearning destabilizes their identity. If everything you believed was shaped by others, then who are you without those beliefs?

I had to unlearn guilt. I had to unlearn fear. I had to unlearn the idea that questioning God was a sin. I had to unlearn the belief that my worth came from obedience. I had to unlearn the programming that told me suffering was noble. Unlearning didn't take me away from God, it brought me closer. I found God in silence, in intuition, in energy, in nature, in myself. Not in rules, not in fear, not in punishment.

Unlearning made room for spiritual evolution. It opened the door to the Universe speaking in ways that religion could not. It taught me that truth is not found in tradition. It is found in alignment.

Transformation of the Universe

Everything in existence evolves, including the Universe itself. Energy shifts, frequencies rise, and spiritual currents move through the world constantly. As an empath, I feel these changes in ways that are sometimes overwhelming. There are days when my energy feels high, as though I'm vibrating on a different plane. Then there are days when everything feels heavy and low, even when I'm eating healthy and doing all the "right" things. That sensitivity is not weakness, it is awareness.

The Universe is going through its own transformation, and those who are spiritually attuned feel the effects without needing explanation. Collective pain, collective healing, collective awakening, all of it touches us. The more I evolved, the more I realized I was moving in rhythm with something bigger than myself. The Universe was shifting, and so was I.

Some moments felt like divine alignment. Synchronicities, intuitive messages, dreams, and insights that revealed parts of my purpose. Other moments felt like breakdowns, where the weight of the world was too much for my spirit to hold. But transformation is not supposed to feel comfortable. It stretches you, challenges you, and demands that you release what no longer fits your soul.

The Universe teaches through cycles. It pushes you into situations until you learn the lesson. It elevates you when you're ready, not when you're comfortable. And as I grew spiritually, I recognized that the changing world wasn't something to fear, it was something to flow with.

Going on Auto

The definition of "auto" is "self," but most people aren't living as themselves. They're living as distractions, expectations, or illusions. So I had to ask: Whose self are we operating as? Are we the self that is influenced by technology? By societal validation? By the opinions of others? Or are we the self that is present, intentional, and aware?

People say they don't want to be part of society's programming, yet they fall right into it. What used to be called being a "sellout" is now being "asleep." Being "woke" isn't about politics, it's about awareness. It's about questioning what everyone else accepts as truth. But true self-reflection can make you sick to your stomach. If it doesn't, you're not doing it deeply enough.

Many people live their lives on autopilot. They drive home without remembering the journey. They walk into a room and immediately forget why they went in. They scroll for hours without ever feeling present. Being disconnected from your surroundings is a symptom of autopilot living. And autopilot is one of the most dangerous states to be in. It steals your awareness and numbs your intuition.

I've been guilty of it too. My husband is the first one to call me out when I'm not mentally present. We made a rule. No phones or technology at the dinner table. It forced us to talk, even on days when talking felt exhausting. It helped us reconnect. People have lost the ability to communicate. They don't know how to sit in silence, how to observe, how to feel the moment without capturing it on a screen.

Meditation helped me retrain my mind. It helped me collect memories intentionally, not artificially through filters and posts. Life is not meant to be lived behind a camera. Life is meant to be lived with presence. When you stop being present, you stop creating memories that matter. And eventually, you start to regret the moments you never truly lived.

Being present saved me. It brought me back to myself. It reminded me that life is not a performance. It is an experience.

As she stripped away old programming, what remained was the raw truth: healing the mind is as essential as healing the spirit. To move forward, Elizabeth had to face the emotional and mental battles she had spent years surviving.

CHAPTER 4

Mind, Trauma, and Self-Sabotage

"Your wound is probably not your fault, but your healing is your responsibility." — Buddha

Emotional wounds often hide in silence. Trauma becomes a shadow we learn to live with, even when it steals our peace. In this chapter, Elizabeth opens the door to her internal world. The battles with anxiety, PTSD, self-doubt, and the patterns that shaped her adulthood. Her honesty here becomes medicine.

My Mental Challenges

"Just breathe, Liz."

That sentence became my lifeline in moments where anxiety felt like it was gripping my chest. For years, I battled with a mind that always prepared for the worst. Even when life was calm, my spirit braced for impact. I thought this was normal, a part of growing up, a part of being a mother, a part of being a woman who had experienced too much too soon. I didn't know my mind was functioning out of survival instead of peace. I didn't know that the trauma I had normalized was shaping the way I interpreted every moment of my life.

My mind learned early that anything could go wrong at any time, so it lived on high alert. I carried the pressure of being prepared for everything, even though life has a way of humbling you and showing you that not everything *can* be prepared for. My moods began shifting more intensely around age thirty. I could be joyful in the morning and at rock bottom by the afternoon. I blamed hormones, age, stress, anything except the truth: that I was carrying decades of unprocessed emotions.

Looking back, I realize I was never taught emotional awareness. In my twenties, I didn't know how to identify a mood swing or understand a trigger. I didn't know that trauma hides inside your body and resurfaces when it feels threatened. As I grew older, these shifts became more extreme. One moment I felt like the strongest woman in the world, and the next, I felt like I was falling apart internally with no explanation.

Culturally, I grew up thinking my emotional battles were demons or spiritual attacks. Any sadness, confusion, or mental fog was labeled as something unholy, something to pray away, something to rebuke. So I prayed with confusion, hoping God would take it away. But when the emotions didn't disappear, I started believing maybe God didn't love me. That's the lie trauma tells you, that you're too broken to be loved.

By age forty, I was diagnosed with PTSD, and suddenly the pieces made sense. Domestic abuse had broken me in ways I didn't want to admit. The shouting, the raised voices, the arguments. They left scars deeper than the bruises. I became terrified of someone raising their voice, especially men. My body remembered every moment of danger, even when my mind tried to move on. Pain has a memory, and mine was loud.

As a mother of sons, I knew the importance of teaching them emotional awareness, especially when interacting with women. I needed them to understand softness, patience, and safe space. A numb woman is not cold, she is wounded. And a woman who has never been given emotional safety cannot magically know how to express herself. Teaching my sons this became a form of healing for myself. I wanted them to grow into men who didn't silence women, but listened to them.

Losing peace of mind helped me understand how priceless it truly is. When your mental state slips, every part of your life is affected. Your sleep, your relationships, your work, your joy. I had been struggling mentally since childhood and never realized how much my own mother's fears shaped mine. She believed I had a mental disability, that I couldn't think for myself, that something was "wrong" with me. She didn't know her protectiveness was turning into emotional restriction. Her fear trickled into me and formed a belief that I wasn't capable.

I became disabled in my own thinking. Not physically, but emotionally. I doubted everything. I second-guessed myself constantly. I feared making decisions. I feared being wrong. And because asthma made my mother overly protective, she unintentionally taught me that the world was dangerous and that I needed her to survive it. She didn't know she was enabling my helplessness; she thought she was loving me.

Life taught me that everyone in your journey is either a tool to sharpen you or a weight to break you. Sometimes they are both. Their purpose isn't always pretty, but it is always essential. My mother taught me caution, but she also taught me resilience. My trauma taught me fear, but it also taught me how to heal.

At forty, I finally sought therapy. Years of holding in trauma, hurt, and pain had formed a thick emotional callus on my spirit. I needed to stop pacifying my hurt, to stop treating it like a blanket I clung to because it felt familiar. Pain can become a comfort zone if you've lived in it long enough. I had convinced myself that I needed my pain to survive, when in reality, all it did was silence my joy.

Therapy showed me a different way. My first therapist was a blessing. Gentle, intuitive, spiritually aligned. She saw me and didn't rush me. She told me therapy was like unpacking a closet: you lay everything out, even the things you forgot were there, and then you choose what to keep and what to release. She created space for me to be honest, to be messy, to be vulnerable. She helped me understand that healing takes radical openness.

Losing my father at forty-four reopened wounds I had tried to avoid. Losing my mother at sixteen froze me emotionally. Watching her take her last breath made me helpless and overwhelmed. I was stuck in that moment for decades. Every loss felt like losing her again. Trauma doesn't keep time, it keeps score.

My mental battles shaped me, but they no longer define me.

The Body Keeps the Score

Trauma is not just an emotional wound, it becomes a physical imprint. The body remembers what the mind tries to forget. It stores fear in your stomach, anxiety in your chest, panic in your breath, and sadness in your muscles. I didn't understand this until I realized that every time I felt triggered, my body reacted before my thoughts did. My heart raced, my chest tightened, and my hands shook even when I told myself I was safe.

The body keeps the score of the moments you survived.
Of the nights you cried silently.
Of the fights you pretended didn't hurt.
Of the words that cut deeper than fists.

The body remembers.

When I entered relationships, my body anticipated abandonment before love even had a chance to grow. When opportunities arrived, my body expected disappointment. When joy showed up, my body prepared for pain. That is what trauma does. It conditions your nervous system to expect danger, even in peace.

Healing required more than talking about my past, it required listening to my body. I had to breathe deeply, move intentionally, and challenge the physical sensations that tried to convince me I was still in danger. Healing wasn't just a mental journey; it was physical liberation.

Self-Sabotage

Self-sabotage is one of the most intimate enemies you'll ever face because it wears your face. It speaks in your voice. It uses your fears as justification. The moments in my life when everything started going right were often the moments I found ways to destroy them. It wasn't intentional, it was protective. My mind believed peace was temporary and happiness was a setup. So I ruined blessings before they could ruin me.

Self-sabotage hides in patterns you dismiss as personality traits. It is the fear of success disguised as humility. It is the fear of love disguised as independence. It is the fear of disappointment disguised as "I don't need anyone." I pushed away opportunities because I didn't trust myself to handle them. I pushed away people because I didn't believe they would stay. I pushed away love because I feared the hurt that follows intimacy.

Healing showed me that self-sabotage is learned behavior. It is childhood pain repeating itself in adult form. When you grow up unseen, you expect invisibility. When you grow up unheard, you silence yourself. When your earliest experiences teach you that love is conditional or inconsistent, you assume every relationship will mirror that lesson.

Self-sabotage wasn't my truth, it was my trauma.

To heal it, I had to confront the parts of me that feared happiness. I had to accept that peace doesn't have to come with pain. I had to rewrite the narrative that good things don't last. I had to learn to trust myself again. And slowly, I did. Healing from self-sabotage isn't about perfection, it's about awareness.

The Best Lie to Ourselves

The greatest lie we tell ourselves is that we are unlovable, unappreciated, stuck, or defined by our upbringing. We say things like:

> *I'm not loved.*
> *I'm not appreciated.*
> *I'm not where I'm supposed to be.*
> *This is just who I am.*

These lies feel true because they come from the voice of old wounds. But the truth is, we are always evolving. Life forces transformation whether we want it or not. Maturity requires divorcing outdated beliefs. Beliefs we inherited from family, culture, trauma, or fear.

When you let go of the lies, you make room for your truth.

I Was Fine With Being a Villain

There was a time when being seen as the villain didn't bother me. In fact, I embraced it because it gave me power. When people misunderstand you, they create stories about you to fit their comfort zones. Someone interrupted my narrative, rewrote it in their own imagination, and suddenly I became the enemy in a story I didn't author.

What hurt most was that the person creating the villain version of me was someone close. Betrayal rarely comes from strangers, it comes from those who know your vulnerability. You walk on thin ice with people who expect perfection but give you none in return. You try to please them, love them, support them, and somehow still become the problem.

I became the villain in my own family simply because I refused to be controlled. I stopped allowing their opinions to define my worth. I stopped dimming my light to make others comfortable. That freedom made them uncomfortable. But one morning, I decided to end the contract of suffering.

I wrote my own decree.
I released myself from their opinions.
I dissolved their projections.
I divorced the version of family that kept me in bondage.

It felt good. Liberating even. Protecting my peace wasn't selfish; it was survival. For years, my family held me hostage to outdated perceptions of who I used to be. They didn't want to acknowledge who I had become. Their competition, jealousy, and misunderstandings formed a weight I no longer wanted to carry.

Their negativity became my motivation. Not to prove them wrong, but to become more of who I am.

My "Why"

My "why" became the anchor of my transformation. It guided how I healed, how I responded, and how I rebuilt myself. My why was simple: I wanted peace more than anything. Not temporary peace, but deep, soul-anchored peace. The kind that doesn't require validation, explanation, or permission.

Struggle had become my norm, so choosing peace felt like rebellion. But I promised myself that I would respect myself enough to stop accepting situations that robbed me of peace. The more you allow, the less others respect you. The more you shrink, the less others see your worth. I was done shrinking.

I am not the scorned woman my past tried to make me.
I am not the defeated daughter who lost her parents too young.
I am not the villain in anyone's story.
I am not validated by people who misunderstand me.
I am not the wounded child who begged for love.
I am not the woman who accepted abuse just to avoid loneliness.

I am an overcomer of everything that tried to destroy me.
I am a generational breaker.
I am a woman of quiet strength and intentional purpose.
I move with grace.

I love deeply.
And I'm no longer afraid of the woman I am becoming.

These are my affirmations.
These are my truths.

Healing the mind led her to confront the body. Its memories, its weight, its survival strategies. The next part of her journey required releasing the version of herself she had carried for decades.

CHAPTER 5

Body, Identity, and Killing the Old Self

"When the old self dies, the soul remembers its power." — Unknown

Transformation isn't just emotional or spiritual, it's physical. Elizabeth's journey with her body reveals years of hurt, coping, comfort, and resilience. This chapter reflects the shedding of an old identity and the courageous birth of a new one.

Who Was That Woman?

Who *was* that woman? I ask myself that question every time I look back at old pictures and see a version of me I barely recognize. Her smile looked steady, but her spirit was exhausted. Her body carried more than weight, it carried secrets, shame, comfort, fear, and a lifetime of emotional bruises that never healed properly. I used to be 357 pounds, and even though I get tired of repeating that part of my story, it remains a defining chapter in my becoming. It was not just my body that felt heavy. It was also my life that did.

At twenty years old, I wasn't just overweight; I was overwhelmed. I struggled with addictions, not just to food but to love. People talk about food addictions like it's a joke "Oh, I love snacks." No. Mine was different. Mine was a relationship. Food was my escape, my comfort, my reward, my silence, my hiding place. When life hurt, I ate. When I felt invisible, I ate. When I wanted to feel loved, I ate. Food didn't judge me, abandon me, disappoint me, or make me prove my worth.

And when it came to love, I wasn't addicted to healthy affection. I was addicted to the idea of being wanted. Of being chosen. Of being kept. I wanted love so badly that I accepted counterfeit versions of it. I mistook being tolerated for being valued and mistaken attention for affection. My identity became tied to being needed, even when it cost me pieces of myself.

Me and food had a strange relationship. I wasn't eating to live; I was eating to forget. Eating was something I had control over, even when everything else felt uncontrollable. I didn't realize that every bite was a conversation with myself. One I didn't want to have out loud.

But behind the weight, behind the fear, behind the pattern, there was a woman who wanted more. She just didn't know how to say it yet.

The Becoming Before the Becoming

Before I ever killed the old version of myself, I had to meet her. Really meet her. The woman buried underneath the weight, the trauma, and the silence. She was hurting, but she was also fighting. She was messy, but she was also magical. I didn't hate her, I just didn't know how to live with her anymore.

Transformation doesn't start with change.

It starts with *awareness*.

And awareness is the most uncomfortable mirror you'll ever look into.

I Killed "Her" (A Confession)

Yes... I killed her.

Let me explain before you call 911.

This is my confession.

Not the spiritual confession people whisper about at church, but the real kind. The kind where you admit you had to become your own assassin.

"DAMNNNNN!! What did I DO!?"

That was my first thought.

I needed her, or at least I thought I did. I believed we were on the same page. I believed she was helping me survive. But somewhere along the line, she started fighting against me. The very woman I had used as armor became the same woman holding me back.

In my mind, it looked like a boxing match.

Me versus her.

The old me versus the becoming me.

In my imagination, she threw elbows, uppercuts, and emotional punches. I thought I had her beat one day and then she came back swinging the next. I was celebrating an emotional "win," thinking I was finally evolving, only to have her knock me back into my old patterns the next morning.

"Why are we fighting when we're the SAME?!"

"We're NOT the same!" I shouted back inside myself.

I must've looked crazy. Fighting invisible battles in public, making a fool of myself emotionally, and then beating myself up on the drive home. I remember driving fast and angry, yelling, "You've messed up my life!" I wasn't talking to anyone else. I was talking to myself.

To clarify.
I didn't kill a person.
I killed a *persona*.

The old Liz.
The one shaped by pain and bitterness.
The one who used anger as a shield.
The one who hurt people before they hurt her.
The one who was angry with God.
The one who confused survival instincts with personality.

So how did I kill her?

I starved her.
I stopped feeding her desire for chaos.
I ignored her demands for attention.
I stopped letting her speak for me.
I denied her the comfort of old habits.

She wasn't the villain. she was my protector.

But at some point, protectors become prison guards.

And I needed to be free.

I stopped using her as my narrative. I stopped telling her story like it was my destiny. I realized something powerful: some people are meant to touch the people around them... but some are meant to touch THE WORLD. And the old me wasn't ready for the world. But the woman being born? Oh, she was.

It always amazed me that strangers loved me more than family. Friends couldn't always understand me. But the world? The world saw something in me my circle didn't. That was my sign: killing her wasn't losing myself. it was releasing myself.

Reflection

Reflection became one of the most intimate parts of my healing journey. Sitting in the mirror, not to fix my hair, adjust my lashes, or smooth my edges, but to see myself. To really see me. I spent years trying to find the version of me that everyone else projected onto me. I tried to find the woman they blamed, the woman they misunderstood, the woman they judged.

But this time, I wasn't looking for flaws or pain.

I was searching for truth.

Truth in my eyes.
Truth in the scars no one sees.
Truth in the silence I carried.
Truth in the strength I denied myself.

Reflection is not always beautiful. It doesn't always bring peace. Sometimes it brings guilt, anger, or grief. But reflection is always necessary. It forces accountability and invites grace. The mirror doesn't lie to you.
It reveals you.

Sitting with myself taught me that beauty doesn't live in perfection. Beauty lives in awareness. In honesty. In courage. In the willingness to face yourself without running away.

As I reflected, I began seeing purpose in

everything. my childhood, my wounds, my losses, my decisions, my scars, my growing edges. Nothing was wasted. Nothing was accidental. Every moment, even the painful ones, shaped the woman I was becoming.

Reflection gave me language for the things I used to avoid.

And through reflection, I finally saw her. The new me.
The woman I prayed for.
The woman I fought for.
The woman I killed for.

The woman I now choose to be every single day.

Rebuilding herself allowed her to love differently. Deeper, wiser, and with intention.

And in that space, she discovered partnership, kingship, and the kind of love that stands beside transformation.

CHAPTER 6

Love, Kingship, and Partnership

"A divine union doesn't complete you—it elevates you." — Yung Pueblo

Partnership is not just romance; it is reflection. It reveals who we are, challenges who we've been, and supports who we are becoming. Elizabeth's journey into love shows the beauty of a relationship built on growth, honesty, and spiritual alignment.

The King I See vs. The Society of a King

This chapter is a revelation. One I didn't just write about, but lived through. The world teaches us what a king is through titles, crowns, and status. Society says a king is a ruler, a man with authority, someone who governs people with absolute or constitutional power. A king is defined by the throne he sits on, the land he owns, the bloodline he comes from. It sounds regal, powerful, prestigious.

But that definition is society's.
Not mine.

Because as a woman, I don't know a king by what he calls himself.
I know a king by how he *moves*.

A man can call himself a king, but if he's moving like a child emotionally, a coward spiritually, or a stranger to integrity, then the title means absolutely nothing. A real king doesn't need to announce he's one, his actions make it clear.

The King I speak of isn't restricted to patriarchy or a throne. He isn't defined by earthly systems or ancient monarchies. The King I know moves in a spirit of calmness. He leads with centeredness. He walks with integrity. Not because it's expected of him, but because it's natural to him. Integrity flows in how he talks, how he treats people, how he carries himself, and how he nurtures the people connected to him.

A king is decisive, not forceful, not controlling, but clear and intentional. He is hardworking and energetic in spirit, not lazy with life. He speaks well, not in fancy words, but with honesty and care. He protects. Though not through aggression, but through presence. He maintains order, not out of ego, but out of responsibility. He blesses others, not for recognition, but because it's who he is.

The world's version of a king is an aesthetic.

My version of a king is a *feeling*.

A true king inspires. He doesn't dictate.
He builds. He doesn't break.
He rises and helps you rise with him.
He stands tall but never stands above you.

The King is an inspiration, not a definition. He is not limited by titles or restricted by society's lens. He is recognized by how he makes you feel: safe, protected, seen, guided, valued.

If a man can make a woman feel cherished, uplifted, and emotionally safe. If he invites her to rise in her queendom, then and only then, is he moving in kingship. A queen doesn't bow to a king; she meets him, side by side. She becomes a reflection of the level of peace, security, and understanding he brings into her life.

Kingship isn't inherited.
Kingship is earned.
Kingship is lived.

And when you meet a man who walks in his kingship, you don't have to ask if he's a king, you feel it in how he loves.

The Transition Into Partnership

Before I met my husband, I did not fully understand that partnership is its own kind of spiritual classroom. We talk about kingship and queenship like they're separate from love, but real partnership requires both. Meeting someone who walks in their wholeness exposes where you are still broken. It reveals the versions of yourself you've buried, the versions you've abandoned, and the versions you've outgrown but still cling to.

Partnership is where your triggers meet their patience.
Where your wounds meet their wisdom.
Where your fears meet their faith.

It's also where the old you tries to fight the new life you're being offered.

A king will see parts of you that you don't want to see in yourself. A queen will challenge a king to rise emotionally. Love at this level requires unlearning survival mode and embracing vulnerability. It asks you to trust someone with the pieces of you that were once used against you. Partnership forces you to grow, not because love demands perfection, but because love demands truth.

Badges "Love" Adams (My Loving Husband)

Badges "Love" Adams. My loving husband. This man loved me through devastation. Not after I healed, not once I improved, not once I became polished or peaceful. But right in the middle of my mess. That is a different kind of love. One that sees the battle you're fighting internally and still chooses you. One that holds your hand even when your spirit is shaking. One that loves you in your shadow long enough for you to walk into your light.

There were three versions of me when he met me.

The real me. the truth, the heart, the woman.

The one who wanted acceptance. The people pleaser, the appeaser, the avoider.

And the one who didn't give a damn. The defense mechanism, the fighter, the protector.

All three belonged to me, and he accepted every version. He didn't force me to hide her. He never made me feel ashamed. He acknowledged her, entertained her when necessary, redirected her when needed, and loved me through every shift. That's what partnership looks like. Being loved through the layers.

But even love has boundaries.
There came a point where my husband had to challenge the parts of me that were getting in my own way. He "checked" the version of me that tried to sabotage the peace we were building. Not through anger, but through love. Through gentle truth. Through reminding me of who I am, not who my trauma taught me to be.

He showed me reality when my fears tried to distort it. He brought clarity when my anxiety brought chaos. I was a walking contradiction. Wanting friends yet pushing people away, desiring connection yet isolating myself, craving intimacy yet guarding myself like a locked safe.

Sometimes I wanted people around me not to uplift me, but to comfort my demons. I wanted them to understand my brokenness instead of holding me accountable for healing it. My husband saw through that. He loved me enough to challenge me.

    Healing exposes relationships.
    Elevation reveals who can go with you and who cannot.
    Some people are seasonal, and the hardest part is accepting when a season ends.

    I struggled deeply with letting people go. I kept individuals around who were no longer aligned with who I was becoming. I held onto relationships that fit the old me, not the evolving me. But as I elevated mentally and spiritually, it became clear that some people were simply not meant to understand me. And that was okay.

    Elevation is a foreign language to the unhealed.
    Transformation is misunderstood by the stagnant.
    Growth looks like arrogance to those who refuse to grow.

    My higher self was beginning to bloom. This self wasn't fueled by trauma. She wasn't reacting from wounds. She wasn't imprisoned by fear. The version of me created by pain lost her power. My higher self stepped forward. Beautiful, present, free.

    She no longer needed validation.
    She no longer entertained dysfunction.
    She no longer carried shame or performed survival.

    She was becoming.

    And my husband?
    He met her.
    He honored her.
    He loved her into existence.

As love grounded her, life delivered revelations that shook her foundation. What came next was an awakening so powerful, it demanded truth, release, and rebirth.

CHAPTER 7

Decompression, Awakening, and Epiphanies

"Rock bottom will teach you lessons that mountaintops never will." — Unknown

Epiphanies don't arrive quietly. They break, shift, and demand transformation. This chapter captures the moments when everything aligned to push Elizabeth deeper into awakening. Here, she confronts her past, listens to intuition, and embraces clarity.

Decompress

Decompression is that sacred moment when I finally sit down, let my mind exhale, and allow my spirit to release everything I've been holding. It's the stillness that forces me to face my "why," not in panic, but in clarity. These are the moments when I unclench my jaw, soften my shoulders, and breathe like someone who finally remembers she's alive. These moments feel like a vacation away from the expectations, the roles, the responsibilities, and the heaviness of simply being human.

Pain has taught me how to decompress. Pain has gifted me with creativity, insight, and strength I didn't even know I possessed. Artists create their greatest work in pain, not because pain is beautiful, but because pain forces you to feel deeply. Pain is a teacher that doesn't ask permission. It shows up, rearranges your life, and demands to be heard.

Sometimes I feel suffocated by my dreams, not because they're bad, but because they're loud. Dreams can be overwhelming when you don't know where to start, when you're scared of failing, or when you've convinced yourself you don't deserve them. My own B.S.. My self-sabotage, my fears, my negative patterns used to bring me more pain than any outside enemy.

>Life is like a big-ass canvas.
>Every decision is a brushstroke.
>Every mistake is texture.
>Every truth is color.
>Every "why" creates meaning.

>For so long I asked myself, "Why?"
>Why was my life like this?
>Why did things happen the way they did?
>Why couldn't I escape the patterns I inherited from childhood?

I was raised in a certain way, and like many people, I accepted those ways without questioning them. But there came a moment when I had to ask: *When will I divorce this way of thinking?* When will I stop blaming my upbringing and start rewriting my foundation?

Because enlightenment, innerstanding, changes everything.

When you start waking up, you realize your foundation wasn't reality. It was programming. It was survival. It was old beliefs, old wounds, old voices echoing in new seasons. Reality isn't what you inherited; it's what you create.

Reality is the moments you remember and learn from, not the ones you let define you.

A bad choice doesn't make a bad life.
A painful chapter doesn't create a painful destiny.

We are not defective. We are evolving.

I used to remember everything as a child because my imagination was golden. Bright, expansive, magical. But somewhere along the journey into adulthood, I forgot the power of that imagination. Trauma dimmed it. Responsibility buried it. Silence muted it.

So, I had to go back and find that little girl.

Not to rescue her, but to reconnect with her.

To understand her.
To stand beside her.
To bring her forward with me.

The woman I killed in Chapter 5?

She wasn't the only version of me that needed to go. There were parts of me that survived pain in unhealthy ways, parts that hurt me long after others stopped. Those parts had to go too.

Some people looked down on me when I was 357 pounds and suddenly trusted me more when I was 170. They thought my weight loss made me whole, but they didn't know I was spiritually worse at 170 than I ever was at 357. My vengeance wasn't the weight loss. It was becoming a woman they couldn't recognize anymore.

Healing isn't about creating a better body.
Healing is about creating a better being.

And through decompressing, I understood something:

Do everything with good intentions. Because good intentions create good outcomes, even if the path gets messy.

I see my Black sisters walking through the world looking angry, tired, or hardened. But I know what's underneath that expression. It's pressure. It's survival. It's exhaustion. It's the weight of always being strong. Decompressing taught me that strength isn't in holding everything together; strength is in letting it go.

The Awakening

One morning, I woke up and something inside me felt different. It didn't scream or shake or demand attention, it whispered. A soft, peaceful whisper that said, "It's time." And for the first time in years, I listened.

I didn't want to fight anymore.
I didn't want to prove myself.
I didn't want to defend who I was or justify how I felt.

I didn't want to carry explanations like weapons, ready to protect myself from judgment.

I just wanted to *be*.

Be free.
Be present.
Be peaceful.
Be aligned.

Awakening isn't becoming someone new, it's remembering who you've always been underneath the noise. Beneath the trauma. Beneath the labels. Beneath the expectations. It's remembering your original form before life touched you too hard.

I realized I'm most powerful when I'm peaceful.
I'm most divine when I'm aligned.
I'm most authentic when I'm silent.

Everything I thought broke me was actually shaping me.
Every pain had purpose.
Every setback had direction.
Every wound was an initiation.

Awakening reminded me that truth isn't found outside of me, it's found within.

Between Awakening and Epiphany

Awakening shows you the truth.
Epiphany forces you to live in it.

Right after awakening, you face yourself in a new light. Things you used to ignore become loud. Things you used to fear become small. Things you used to misunderstand suddenly become clear. Awakening opens your eyes, but epiphany opens your path.

It's the bridge between "I'm changing" and "I must change."
Between awareness and action.
Between knowing and becoming.

An awakening gives you a choice.
An epiphany makes you choose.

The Epiphany

I was told to be silent during this part of my journey. I felt a summons in my spirit, a pull, a weight that said, "This experience was not just for you." Writing these words makes tears hit the screen because the memory still carries electricity. The moment is still alive inside me.

I was...
but the sentence could never finish without shaking.

Because some epiphanies don't whisper.
They break you open.

I walked into my bedroom one day, and it hit me like a flash. Like lightning ran through my spine. My eyes filled with tears as I remembered that night. A woman stepping in front of my car, an image burned into my mind, an accident that became a wound, a punishment, a trauma I couldn't explain.

I couldn't stop in time. My head spun with confusion, guilt, fear, and disbelief. For ninety days, I had to pay for something that felt like an accident on the outside but was a storm on the inside. Those ninety days weren't about punishment. They were about confrontation.

All of it brought back the deaths I had witnessed.

The goodbyes I never said.
The trauma I buried instead of healing.

I was angry with God.
I tried to negotiate my way out of it.
I felt trapped in a hell I didn't believe I deserved.

In those lowest moments, I had to ask myself, "What did I do to deserve this?" But the real epiphany wasn't about blame. It was about truth. The truth was that I ignored my gut that night. I felt I should've stayed home. I felt something was off. And ignoring that intuition cost me the peace I was already struggling to hold.

The epiphany was that I was the issue. Not because I was bad, but because I didn't trust myself. That accident wasn't who I was, it was a moment. And even though it shook my life, it did not break me.

I didn't fold.
I didn't lose myself.
I didn't let shame destroy me.

I chose to use the experience as a lesson.
Not as a pity story.
Not as a victim narrative.
Not as a curse.

But as clarity.

Our decisions become prisons when we hold guilt longer than we should. We become our own enemy when we fear trusting ourselves again.

I danced in guilt for too long.
I replayed the moment until it became a nightmare.
I punished myself more than any institution ever could.

But when I made the conscious decision to live in the *Now*, to be present, to allow myself to heal, I became free of that past. I became a hero to my future.

My biggest battle wasn't the accident, it was how people saw me afterward.

How they judged me without knowing me.

How they made my accident my identity.

I realized I could never control their perception.

I could only control my truth.

People sit front-row in your life waiting for a downfall. Promoting your failure, hoping for your collapse, hungry for your drama. I refused to let my life become their entertainment. Not on social media, not in gossip circles, not in whispered conversations.

My life is my own.
I am the artist.
And my decisions are my brushstrokes.

Facing Your Giant

Giants aren't always monsters.
Sometimes they're memories.
Sometimes they're fears.

Sometimes they're beliefs we inherited but never questioned.

My giants were fear of success and fear of failure. Two enemies that look different but feel the same. Success scared me because I feared falling. Failure scared me because I feared judgment. So I lived in the space between. Stagnation.

Facing my giants meant entering my little girl space.
Reading my story back to myself.
Confronting the shadows I ignored.
Owning the decisions I hid behind.

I realized all of the pacifying, settling, avoiding, shrinking, that I was doing kept me locked in a room called *stagnation*. A room that felt safe because it was familiar but suffocating because it was small.

My fears came from my perception of success.
Success meant being seen.
Being seen meant being judged.
Being judged meant possibly being abandoned.

I feared becoming a "sell-out," feared losing myself, feared choosing something greater than my comfort zone. But everyone becomes a sell-out at some point, because selling out isn't about fame; it's about selling your old self to buy your new one.

I was tired of wasting energy trying to belong.

Belonging was draining.
Validation was draining.
People-pleasing was draining.

So I wrote this book for the ones who feel unreachable.

For the ones drowning in silence.

For the ones who feel alone in a crowded room.

One giant I faced was church folks. The ones who questioned why I "left God." But the truth?

I didn't leave God.

I left the organization of the church.

I left systems that controlled instead of healed.

I left doctrines that boxed God into fear and shame.

I wasn't programmed to live systematically.

I refused to let religion silence my evolution.

Giants don't disappear, you just outgrow them.
Giants don't die, you can only rise above them.
And once you name your giant, the Universe gives you every tool you need to defeat it.

Meditate on this.
Quiet your mind.
Face your giants.
Your freedom is waiting.

After every storm comes stillness. And in that stillness, Elizabeth heard something she had never heard before: her own frequency.

CHAPTER 8

Channeling My Own Frequency

"When you tune into your own vibration, you become unstoppable." — Lalah Delia

Alignment is not a moment; it's a lifestyle. This chapter reflects the version of Elizabeth who emerged after pain, awakening, and transformation. A woman anchored in her truth, guided by intuition, and walking fully in her power.

My Channeling

The day I stepped outside and felt the wind hit my face, something in me shifted. It wasn't just a breeze moving across my skin; it felt intentional, almost as if the Universe was nudging me forward. Each step toward my car didn't feel ordinary. It felt symbolic, like I was physically walking out of who I used to be and easing into the woman I had been quietly growing into. Growth brings discomfort, and that day I felt all of it, but I also sensed a strange kind of permission. It was as if the uneasiness was telling me, "You're moving in the right direction."

For the first time in years, my energy wasn't wrapped around pain or fear. I wasn't replaying the old stories that used to run my life. I wasn't shrinking to fit anyone else's comfort. I felt myself tuning into a frequency that belonged entirely to me, the woman beneath the layers of noise, obligation, and emotional armor. She had been waiting for air, and that day, she finally breathed.

Becoming My Own Sound

There came a point in my healing where I realized I had stopped borrowing my identity from the expectations of others. I didn't need to filter myself through anyone else's lens anymore. My life no longer echoed chaos or survival; it had begun to develop its own rhythm. Steady, grounded, unmistakably *mine*. I understood then that personal energy speaks long before words do. When a woman is aligned within herself, peace becomes something she carries, not something she searches for.

Feeling at home in myself was new. It was quiet, but not empty, full, but not overwhelming. And as that internal shift settled in, everything around me started feeling different too. Conversations felt more intentional. Connections felt more selective. Even my expectations changed. It wasn't because my circumstances magically improved. It was because I was no longer living from the same place.

Stepping Onto My Own Stage

For most of my life, I played roles other people cast me in. I tried to be the dependable daughter, the caretaker, the protector, the fixer, the "strong one." I learned how to stay composed so others wouldn't have to face their own chaos. But healing eventually taught me that I also deserved a space where I didn't have to perform.

Creating that space took time, tears, and a lot of letting go, but it became sacred. My voice started sounding like my own instead of an echo of responsibility. My identity stopped feeling borrowed. My presence stopped apologizing. And for the first time, I understood that I didn't need applause, permission, or outside validation to own my place in the world.

Standing on a stage built by my own growth means I don't wait to be chosen. I choose myself. I create my narrative, and I stand behind it. I am both the storyteller and the one being transformed by the story.

Vibration Over Validation

Learning to live by vibration instead of validation was one of the most freeing transitions of my life. Validation can feel supportive in the moment, but when you rely on it, you lose your connection to the voice inside you. Vibration, on the other hand, is honest. It doesn't dress itself up. It doesn't need to be approved or accepted. It simply is.

As my vibration changed, I noticed the people around me differently. Some relationships began to fade; not because of conflict, but because they no longer resonated with who I was becoming. Some people were operating from fear, jealousy, insecurity, or emotional survival, and they simply couldn't understand the peace I had started to cultivate. And I had to learn that their misunderstanding wasn't my assignment.

Rising means releasing.
Growing means outgrowing.
Healing means accepting that not everyone will walk with you into your next season.

Some connections are meant to teach you something, not accompany you forever.

Channeling Isn't Magic. It's Mastery

People love to talk about manifestation as if it's something mystical, but real channeling is discipline. It's the quiet choices you make daily, especially when no one is watching. It's how you respond to yourself when fear shows up, how you speak to yourself when doubt whispers, how you move when old patterns try to pull you back.

Channeling your frequency means refusing to abandon yourself the moment things get uncomfortable. It means listening to your intuition instead of the voices that once defined you. It means choosing honesty over habits, alignment over approval, presence over performance. It's a practice. One that becomes a lifestyle the more you honor who you truly are.

Walking in Wind

When the wind hit my face that day, I

understood it differently. Life will always bring movement. Unexpected shifts, sudden changes, redirections you didn't plan for. But when you're aligned with your own frequency, even those disruptions carry meaning.

The wind wasn't chaos; it was clarity.
It wasn't pushing me away; it was pointing me forward.
It wasn't an interruption; it was instruction.

As I crossed that parking lot, the wind felt like a message that I was stepping into a new season, even if I didn't feel fully prepared. Sometimes fear and evolution sit in the same room, and growth doesn't wait until you feel ready. We learn as we walk. We heal as we step. We evolve as we breathe.

That day, the wind's message was simple:
You're becoming the woman you were always meant to be.

The Frequency of Freedom

Freedom quietly changes the way you

move through the world. It softens your breath. It lightens your choices. It releases you from the need to explain yourself. Freedom isn't dramatic or loud, it's grounded. It's peaceful. It's consistent.

Freedom looks like speaking without shrinking, leaving without guilt, loving without losing yourself, growing without waiting for approval, and resting without feeling like you must earn it. It's the moment you stop fighting for room and start creating your own space. It's the moment joy becomes familiar instead of rare.

True freedom is recognizing that what is meant for you doesn't require you to chase it, it will meet you where you stand.

The Creator in Me

For a long time, I believed creation was something that happened outside of me. A gift given by God or the Universe to a chosen few. But the more I healed, the more I realized that creation is internal. We create through every decision we make, every boundary we set, every truth we honor, every wound we choose to heal instead of hide.

> My life is something I built.
> My identity is something I shaped.
> My peace is something I protected.

I don't wait for miracles anymore because I understand now that becoming is a miracle in itself. I don't look for breakthroughs. I live in the breakthrough. I don't wait to be chosen, I recognize I was never unchosen to begin with.

Channeling my own frequency taught me that the very things I was searching for were inside me the entire time. They were just waiting for me to stop dimming and start listening.

The Final Note

This may be the last chapter of the book, but it isn't the end of who I'm becoming. If anything, it is the beginning of a new rhythm I get to walk in. Every loss, every shift, every awakening, every moment of silence and reflection brought me here, to this clarity, this alignment, this truth.

> I am no longer shaped by trauma.
> I am shaped by choice, by intention, by awareness, by grace.

> I am not the woman I had to survive as.
> I am the woman I chose to become.

> I am my own frequency now. steady, grounded, divine.

> And for the first time in my life,
> I finally sound like myself.

Every chapter of Elizabeth's life built the foundation for the woman she stands as today. Rooted, intentional, evolving, and free. Her story does not end here; it expands. Because once a woman learns her own frequency, she becomes her own liberation.

Paintings by Elizabeth

These Paintings

COURAGE

勇

霊
Spiritual

仁
Compassion

礼
RESPECT

エリサ
Elizabeth
24

Creative
Patient
Innovative
Loving
Strong
Queen
Amazing
Sexy
Beautiful
Positive
Smart
Enough
Resilient

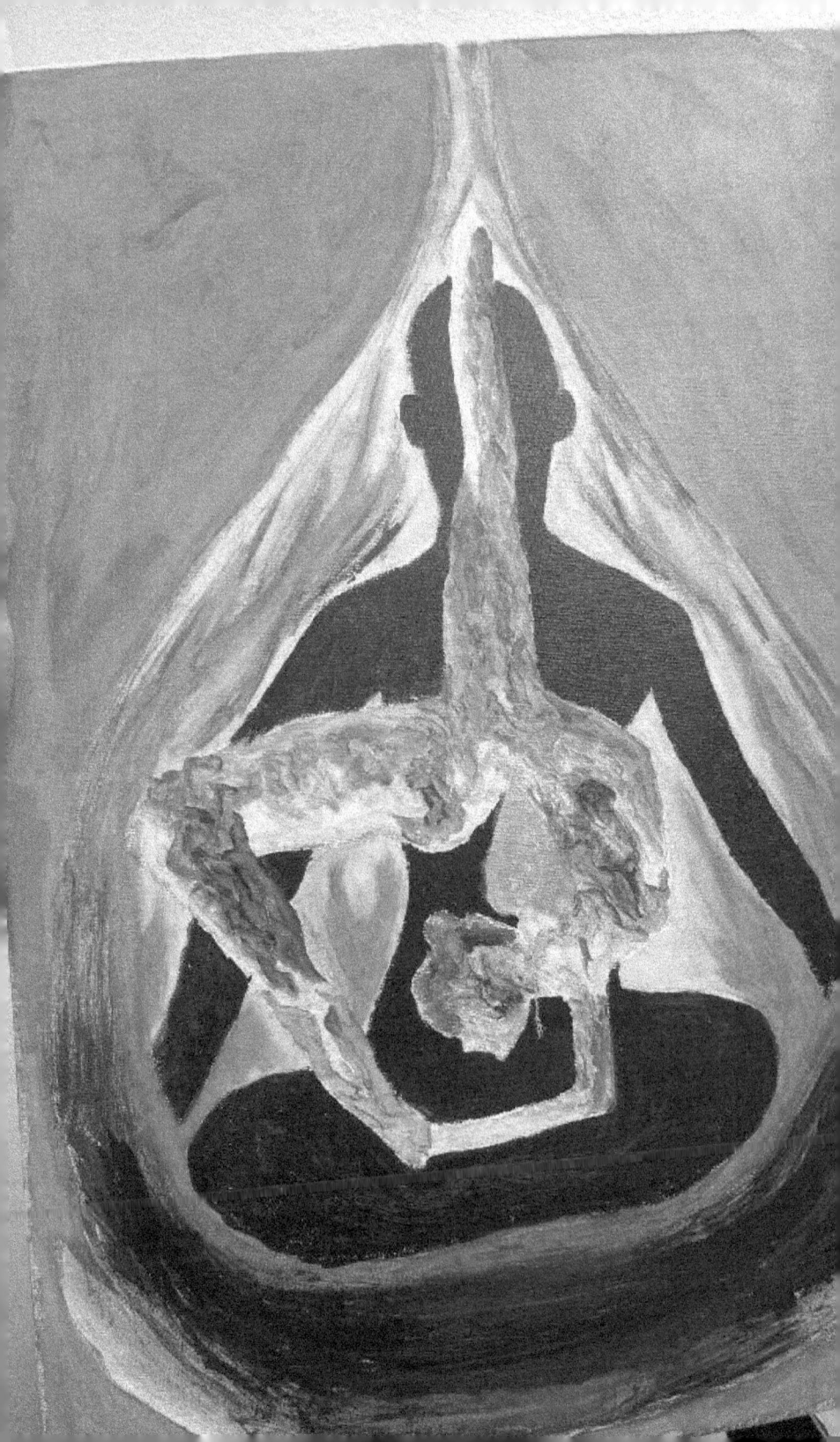

www.ingramcontent.com/pod-product-compliance
Lightning Source LLC
Chambersburg PA
CBHW021013090426
42738CB00007B/775